PRAIRIE FIRE!

The Folklore and Natural History of The American Grasslands

By
Brian "Fox" Ellis

Fox Tales International presents
Fox Tales Folklore
**A Series of Ecological, International
and American Folklore**

Other Books in the Fox Tales Folklore Series :
Tall Tree Tales
A River of Stories
Bird Tales
Fox Tales
Fish Tales
Fun with Fables
Celtic Tales
River Ghosts
Speaking Truth to Power
In A Spring Garden

*Each book in the series is available as an ebook,
paperback, audio-book, podcast and video!*

*Please contact Fox for wholesale orders,
library and school discounts.*
foxtales@foxtalesint.com

*Cover art, book design, and interior illustrations
by Devin McSherry.*
www.devinmcsherry.com

Fox Tales International

Presents

PRAIRIE FIRE!

The Folklore and Natural History of
The American Grasslands

**Researched, Written, Edited and Performed
by Brian "Fox" Ellis**

**Fox Tales International
P.O. Box 209
Bishop Hill, IL 61419
www.foxtalesint.com**

PRAIRIE FIRE!
by Brian "Fox" Ellis

Table of Contents

PRAIRIE FIRE!
A Poem for Three Voices

One: The never-ending ocean of waving grasses,

Two: this flowing sea of flowers and fluttering field
        of butterflies

Three: catches spark and blazes.

Two: A Prairie Fire!

One: A Prairie Fire!

All: A Prairie Fire!

Three: 300 million years burn away
        and the ocean of grasses turns to ash.

One: A real sea rises and falls
        laying down the bedrock of the prairie to come.

Two: A great sea of ice slowly creeps down from the north
        giving off an eerie glow of cold fire.

One: The glacier grinds stones to sand,
        carries huge boulders hundreds of miles
        and leaves them tumbled about a barren tundra.

Three: This bedrock of limestone

Two: and the ground down glacial erratics

One: provide the fertility to grow an ocean of grasses.

Two: A thousand years of heat and drought
        pushes back the glaciers and conifers,

One: Wooly mammoth and mastodon,

Three: Saber toothed cat and sloth bear,
        dire wolf and bison giganticus

One: Creatures great and small move into these fertile fields
        and forests,

Two: followed by homo-sapiens, the first humans.

Three: CRACK! Lightening strikes the tallest oak in the savannah

1

Two: A Prairie Fire!

One: A Prairie Fire!

All: A Prairie Fire!

Two: Humans learn to make tools,

Three: arrow heads and spear points,

One: stone axes, bows and arrows,

Three: and fire becomes a tool.

Two: The people learn to drive the herds of bison off a cliff
with the aid of fire.

One: The plants become fire adaptive.

Two: The fire clears away the duff and converts it to ash.

One: The ash is fertilizer.

Three: Even ta-tanka, the buffalo, learns to love the fire,
for the fertile green shoots that sprout after the fire has
passed becomes their favorite food.

Two: As the people sit round the cooking fire,
feasting on the flesh of buffalo,

One: prairie grasses converted to meat,

Two: they tell the tales of not so long ago,

One: not so far away.

(You can share this poem with two friends. Each of the three of you choose a number and take turns reading the parts out loud.)

THE WOMAN WHO LIVED WITH THE WOLVES
A True Story from the Lakota

Many long winters ago, the Lakota would follow the great herds of bison through the summer, but as summer moved towards autumn, the people would gather for their annual fall hunt. Working together, half of the village would spread out on the prairie surrounding a herd of Tatanka, the buffalo. When the signal was given they would set fire to the prairie and create a wall of flames to herd the buffalo. One of the fastest and bravest members of the tribe would run into the herd and harass one of the old bulls, one of the buffalo elders. The goal was to get the buffalo to chase them!

The buffalo would flee the flames. The wall of fire would chase the buffalo towards a cliff. Some folks call the fire the red buffalo. The young person would whoop and holler, leading the herd. The buffalo would chase them. They would lead them to the cliff. You had to be fast or you could be trampled by the herd. When they arrived at the cliff's edge they would step down onto a small ledge they knew was there. Then they would roll against the cliff as the herd came careening over the top.

The buffalo would quickly pile up at the bottom of the cliff.

The rest of the village would be waiting in the valley. They would butcher the bison, smoke and dry the meat, tan the hides, and have a huge feast to fatten up for the coming winter. The buffalo would provide for the people. Their flesh was our food. Their fur would make our coats and cover our lodges. Their bones made our tools. The tendons and sinew would be used as thread to sew the leather. The brains would be used to tan the hides. Every animal has just enough brains to tan its own hide. A horn could be carved into a spoon or a comb. A stomach or bladder would make a canteen or storage vessel. Every part of the buffalo was used. The buffalo gave its life so the people could live. The Lakota respected this life.

After the fall hunt, before the first snows, the people would move towards their winter camp. It is hard to travel and hard to hunt when the snow is deep upon the prairie. So they would hope to have enough and more than enough to make it through the winter.

Among the people there was a young girl who had one thing she loved more than anything else. Arf, Arf! It was her puppy. Arf, Arf! Everywhere she went her puppy went with her. As the people were moving towards their winter camp, this girl helped her mother load things onto her travois. If you think about it, a tipi was the first mobile home. The Lakota would take down their tipi, lay the buffalo robes over the frame, tie two poles together and lay that over their shoulders. This was called a travois, actually a French word for trailer.

On a good day they might make five or six miles. On a great day they might travel eight or ten miles. On this day they covered five miles before lunch and another five after. But when they stopped for lunch, the young woman did not see her puppy. She asked her friends, *"Have you seen my puppy?"*

They said, *"No, we have not seen your puppy since this morning."*

"Have you seen my puppy?"

"No, I have not seen your puppy since yesterday."

Without telling her mother where she was going, this young woman thought maybe her puppy was lost and decided to retrace their steps to see if she could find her dog. At first it was easy to follow the footsteps of a hundred people dragging their travois, but then the first snow of the season began to fall. The snow began to fill in the footprints. But on the open prairie, you can see for miles. The young woman could see the cliff, near the river, where they had chased the buffalo over the edge. They had camped there for several days as they were tanning the hides. She thought she might find her puppy there, gnawing on the bones.

When she arrived at this place, she did not find her puppy. Now, the snow was falling thickly. The girl was cold, tired and hungry. She knew darkness was coming. She remembered there were some small caves along the edge of the cliff. She thought, if I could only get out of the snow and the cold. She crawled along the edge of the cliff, but she did not just climb into the cave. No, she was smarter than that. She knew that these caves could be home to a cougar or bear, wolves or coyotes. Sniff, sniff. First she smelled the cave. If a bear or wolf lived there you would smell them! It did not smell like anyone was home.

Only when she felt safe did she climb inside the cave. Inside she could not see, but she could feel. The cave was not big enough to stand up, but it was long enough to lie down and she did. Soon she was asleep.

Meanwhile back in the village, when the people stopped for lunch, the mother did not worry that she did not see her daughter. It does take a village to raise a child. The mother figured that her daughter was having lunch with her Aunt and some of her friends. But when they stopped for the night and she did not see her daughter, the mother was at first angry.

"There are chores to be done and she is not here. She is shirking her responsibility!" But as she began to look for her daughter, she sensed that something was not right. Every mother's worst fear, her daughter had disappeared. She began to ask the young woman's friends, *"Have you seen my daughter?"*

"No, I have not seen her since we stopped for lunch," they said.

"Have you seen my daughter?"

"No, I have not seen her since this morning," said a friend.

Every mother's worst nightmare, you do not want to imagine...

Quickly they organized a search party. Several people without their heavy burdens could retrace those ten miles in a matter of hours. When they arrived at the place where they had stopped for lunch, they saw the little girl's footprints heading back towards where they had chased the buffalo off the cliff. They ran on, but the snow began to fill in the footprints, and the sun set. Luckily, it was a full moon night and the moon reflecting on the snow allowed them to travel. On the open prairie, you can see for miles. They could see the cliff, near the river, where they had chased the buffalo over the edge. They ran on.

When they arrived at their camp, they found fresh tracks in the snow, but not the tracks of a little girl. These were the tracks of wolves...and there was blood. They feared the worst. They traveled on through the night until they arrived back at their village. They told the mother what they had seen.

Oh, the grief. You don't want to imagine, every mother's worst nightmare. Her little girl was gone! As is the custom among the Lakota, she would have shaved her head and smeared ashes in her face, like a death mask, she wore her grief. So when she cried day and night people knew that she had lost a child... but the little girl was okay. You know that, she was sleeping in a cave, but the mother did not know.

Somewhere in the middle of the night the little girl woke up. She remembered a strange dream in which she was surrounded by a pack of wolves. She was scared, but the wolves sensed her fear and the alpha female, the big mama, whined and whimpered, as if to say, *"Do not be afraid. You were lost, but we have found you. You were alone, but we will take care of you."* When the girl felt a warm, wet tongue on her check she woke up. Staring a wolf in the eye she quickly realized this was not a dream. She was afraid, but the wolf sensed her fear and whined, whimpered. The girl remembered her dream and she knew what this meant. The big mama wolf, the leader of the pack, alpha female, curled up around her and the girl went back to sleep. It was the middle of the night.

In the morning when she awoke there were no wolves. Maybe it was a dream. (Sniff-sniff.) It did not smell like a dream. The cave smelled like wolves! She was tired from the long journey of the previous day. She had slept late. When she crawled out of the cave the sun was bright, the world was white, the snow had fallen on and off throughout the night. Coming across the now frozen river, the girl saw a pack of wolves and stiffened with fear. The wolves sensed her fear and stopped, except the alpha female. She brought a chunk of raw meat, liver from wapiti, the elk.

Now put yourself in her moccasins. When you are really, really hungry, you can admit it, do you eat things you do not usually eat? She had no breakfast, it was lunch time, she had no supper, she left before lunch the day before. She was really hungry. She knew liver from a healthy animal is the healthiest part. She ate.

From that day on the wolves cared for her. Every night when she went to bed the alpha female would curl up around her to keep her warm. But wolves are nocturnal. They hunt at night. This meant that every morning when she awoke there was fresh meat. She lived with the wolves all winter long. She began to learn the language of wolves.

Wolf language is actually a lot like human language, it is mostly body language. Think about it: the way you sit, stand and walk says something about what you think about yourself and how you relate to your world. The same is true with wolves. Dogs are wolves. When a dog wants in or out it scratches on the door. When it wants petted it roles over so you will rub its belly. Wolves communicate in much the same way.

When the girl had a piece of meat and a big wolf wanted it, this wolf would puff herself up, stiffen her tail, bare her teeth and growl. Saying loud and clear, *"Give it to me or else!"* Of course she would share; it was their meat to begin with.

If a small wolf wanted the piece of meat, this wolf would hunker down, tuck his tail under his legs, bare his gums and tongue, whimpering, *"Please share with me, please."* Of course she would share, please usually works.

She loved to sit on a hillside and listen to the wolves howl. When the whole pack howls they can be heard up to five miles away on the open prairie.

Finally, the snows began to melt and the spring flowers began to bloom.

One night, she was sitting on a hillside listening to the wolves howl, when they said something she did not at first understand. They were asking about the village of two legged animals... they were talking about her village. In the morning the alpha female came to her and said, g-r-r-r, g-r-r-r... OR prepare for a long journey. We shall travel for four days and four nights without rest. Eat all you can. The girl did as she was told. She ate and drank all her belly could hold. The truth is a pack of wolves can run 200 miles without rest. She could not keep up. Every now and then they would stop and let her rest a short bit before rousing her and pushing her onwards.

On the fourth morning they came to the top of a hill and there in the valley she saw her village. At the edge of the village she saw her mother's lodge. She knew it was her mother's lodge from the paintings on the buffalo hides AND she saw her mother coming out of the lodge.

She was torn. She wanted to run down and give her mother a big hug, but she did not want to leave her new family. She fell to her hands and knees. Whimpering, she begged the wolves to come with her to greet her other family. Most of the wolves growled their response making it clear that they would not feel welcome. The people do not like us. She whined, she begged, please, please, I will tell them what you have done for me. But the wolves growled and scowled, some people will not understand; we can not go with you.

She was torn. What would you do? Live with the wolves or run down the hill to give your mother a big hug? She gave each of the wolves a big hug and thanked them in their language. But then she stood up. She was, after all, a two-legged animal. She walked down the hill to see her mother.

Her mother rubbed her eyes in disbelief. Her daughter was gone! But it did not run like a ghost. It did not sound like a ghost. It did not feel like a ghost. Mother and daughter embraced. The village heard the commotion and ran to see. When the father saw his daughter he picked up both his wife and the young woman and swung them both around. Then the young woman, for now she was clearly a woman, she told them the story of the wolves, the winter, and the wonderful care she received.

At first some people were not sure, could this be true? A hunter said, "Since the wolves fed you all winter the least we could do is to feed the wolves. This morning I brought home a deer. I cannot eat the bones and scraps. I will offer them to the wolves." Another hunter stepped forward and said, *"Yesterday, I brought home wapiti, an elk, I cannot eat the scraps and bones. I, too, offer these to feed the wolves."*

The girl went about the village with a deer skin, gathering bones and scraps, until she had such a large bundle of meat she could not carry it. She dragged this bundle of food to the top of the hill. The whole village watched as the wolves came out of hiding and greeted her like family. They knew this story to be true.

From that day on, wherever the village of two legged animals went, the village of four legged animals followed. If the people chased a herd of buffalo off of a cliff the wolves would also eat their fill. The wolves also helped the people. If the herd of buffalo headed off in a new direction the wolves would call out, howl, and tell the girl, who would tell the hunters and the village never went hungry again.

Eventually this young woman grew up and grew old. Eventually she crossed over to the other world. But the people say that sometimes at night if you listen closely, when you hear the wolves howl, sometimes you will hear the old woman howl, the old woman who lived with the wolves.

BUFFALO BROTHERS
by Luther Standing Bear

At one time great fields of the golden sunflower grew on the plains of the Sioux country. Both the Sioux and the buffalo loved this beautiful flower. Its leaves were so bright and green and the yellow petals more lovely and delicate than gold.

Many little yellow birds, so many they could not be counted, hovered over the fields of sunflowers. They loved the sunflower, too, and their feathers were almost as yellow as the petals arranged so neatly around the centers of brown. The birds picked at these brown seeds and talked a lot while they were about it. No wonder, then, that we boys liked to lie around on pleasant days in these fields and take in all the sights and sounds. Everything interested us.

The buffalo liked to wallow their big heads in the sunflowers, and many times we saw them with long stems wound about the left horn, for they never wore them on the right horn. Perhaps they did this to decorate themselves, or maybe they liked the smell of the flowers. We only knew that they liked the sunflower.

Of course, we boys did not try to get very close to the buffalo, but we sat on our ponies at a distance and watched them. In the summer, if the flies were bad, the buffalo raised the dust with their horns and the dust-clouds would hide them from us for a while. Sometimes we saw them play, and sometimes we saw them swim in a lake with only their big black heads above the water. From a distance it looked like a single moving black body on the surface of the water.

One day a great hunt took place. The braves killed many buffalo and brought home many hides.

The next day some of us boys rode out on the prairie. No buffalo were in sight. Everything was quiet except the birds in the sunflower fields. I rode alone up a little hill, and looking over, saw two buffalo. I was surprised, for I thought that they had all been killed or had been frightened away. I sat on my pony and watched. One buffalo was on the ground, his feet under him; the other was nosing and pushing the fallen one about with his head and horns. I was curious, and watched for several moments before I realized that the buffalo on the ground was either ill or wounded. The day before, no doubt, he had been wounded, but had been able to escape the hunters. At this spot he had lain down weak from the loss of blood. With the grunted urges of the helpful buffalo, the wounded one would try to rise. Each time he tried, he got upon his forefeet, but each time sank back again. However, this seemed to be satisfactory, for the friendly buffalo moved on.

The next day my curiosity brought me back to the place, but I came alone. The wounded buffalo still sat on the ground. After I had waited for an hour or so, I saw the other buffalo coming. When he got to the wounded one, there was a greeting with horns and heads. The well buffalo encouraged the sick one with rubbing and poking, and pushing him with his head. The poor fellow rose to his feet and stood for a moment, but sank back to the ground again. The second time he got to his feet he walked for a few steps and again lay down. But he was in a clean place and there was some green grass close by. In a little while the visiting buffalo went back to his herd somewhere in the distance and out of sight.

I could not now help going back to see what was to happen, so the next day I was looking on again. The unfailing friend came as before, and the stricken buffalo must have revived considerably, for after some coaxing he arose on weakened legs, but followed his friend away at a slow but steady pace.

I saw them disappear, and I went home feeling that I had been made better by this lesson in kindness.

THE PRAIRIE DOGS AND THE RAIN
An Apache Folktale

We know that the wild creatures who share our home are attuned to changes in the weather. They know when to hunker down, when a storm is coming. They have been seen fleeing an area before a flood. An architect recently designed a more energy efficient building based on prairie dog ventilation systems. A National Geographic researcher has been studying prairie dog language. Maybe if we humbled ourselves and paid more attention to the things other creatures know we could learn a thing or two from the four-legged, the winged, the creepy-crawly, and the green people who share our world. This old Apache story speaks of such knowing.

Many long years ago there was a young, inexperienced hunter out wandering on the prairie. He spent so much time following the tracks of his prey that he soon had trouble following his own tracks to find his way home. It was an extremely hot summer day. He was soon thirsty beyond measure. We know that when you lose just 5% of your moisture you lose 20% of your strength and stamina. This young man soon became delirious with thirst. He threw down his bow and arrows. He dropped all of his burdens. He wandered aimlessly. He eventually fell to his knees and crawled along, desperate for water.

When he realized he was in a prairie dog village he knelt beside a prairie dog hole and he begged for mercy. He begged for water. *"Please little brothers and sisters, can you help me?"*

16

A small prairie dog came out of its burrow with an even smaller vessel of water. The young man did not think this would parch his thirst, but he drank. He drank and drank and he could not empty the small cup.

His strength returned to him, as did a clearer mind. He thanked the prairie dog for saving his life. The little prairie dog said, *"Follow your footsteps. Pick up your bow and arrows, and continue to walk in the direction from where you have come. Find your way back to your village and you will find water. The little people will help you find more water."*

The young man did as he was told. He found his things. He found his way home. As he neared his village he saw rain clouds gathering over the mountains in the distance. He could smell the fresh scent of rain wafting on the cooling breeze. He saw the small streams swell with the run-off from the mountains. He knew the prairie dogs had sent the rain.

If you ever find yourself lost in the western short grass prairies look to the prairie dogs, humble yourself before them, and they might teach you a thing or two about living in this arid land.

THE PRAIRIE - 1811
By John James Audubon

ON my return from the Upper Mississippi, I found myself obliged to cross one of the wide Prairies, which, in that portion of the United States, vary the appearance of the country. The weather was fine, all around me was as fresh and blooming as if it had just issued from the bosom of nature. My knapsack, my gun, and my dog, were all I had for baggage and company. But, although well moccasined, I moved slowly along, attracted by the brilliancy of the flowers, and the gambols of the fawns around their dams, to all appearance as thoughtless of danger as I felt myself.

My march was of long duration; I saw the sun sinking beneath the horizon long before I could perceive any appearance of woodland, and nothing in the shape of man had I met with that day. The track which I followed was only an old Indian trace, and as darkness overshadowed the prairie, I felt some desire to reach at least a copse of trees, in which I might lie down to rest. The Night-hawks were skimming over and around me, attracted by the buzzing wings of the beetles which form their food, and the distant howling of wolves gave me some hope that I should soon arrive at the skirts of some woodland.

I did so, and almost at the same instant a fire-light attracting my eye, I moved towards it, full of confidence that it proceeded from the camp of some wandering Indians. I was mistaken:—I discovered by its glare that it was from the hearth of a small log cabin, and that a tall figure passed and re-passed between it and me, as if busily engaged in household arrangements.

I reached the spot, and presenting myself at the door, asked the tall figure, which proved to be a woman, if I might take shelter under her roof for the night. Her voice was gruff', and her attire negligently thrown about her. She answered in the affirmative. I walked in, took a wooden stool, and quietly seated myself by the fire. The next object that attracted my notice was a finely formed young Indian, resting his head between his hands, with his elbows on his knees. A long bow rested against the log wall near him, while a quantity of arrows and two or three raccoon skins lay at his feet. He moved not; he apparently breathed not. Accustomed to the habits of the Indians, and knowing that they pay little attention to the approach of civilized strangers. I addressed him in French, a language not infrequently partially known to the people in that neighborhood. He raised his head, pointed to one of his eyes with his finger, and gave me a significant glance with the other. His face was covered with blood. The fact was, that an hour before this, as he was in the act of discharging an arrow at a raccoon in the top of a tree, the arrow had split upon the cord, and sprung back with such violence into his right eye that it was destroyed forever.

Feeling hungry, I inquired what sort of fare I might expect. Such a thing as a bed was not to be seen, but many large untanned bear and buffalo hides lay piled in a corner. I drew a fine time-piece from my breast, and told the woman that it was late, and that I was fatigued. She had spied my watch, the richness of which seemed to operate upon her feelings with electric quickness. She told me that there was plenty of venison and jerked buffalo meat, and that on removing the ashes I should find a cake. But my watch had struck her fancy, and her curiosity had to be gratified by an immediate sight of it. I took off the gold chain that secured it from around my neck, and presented it to her. She was in ecstasy, spoke of its beauty, asked me its value, and put the chain round her brawny neck, saying how happy the possession of such a watch should make her. Thoughtless, and, as I fancied myself, in so retired a spot, secure, I paid little attention to her talk or her movements. I helped my dog to a good supper of venison, and was not long in satisfying the demands of my own appetite.

The Indian rose from his seat, as if in extreme suffering. He passed and re-passed me several times, and once pinched me on the side so violently, that the pain nearly brought forth an exclamation of anger. I looked at him. His eye met mine; but his look was so forbidding, that it struck a chill into the more nervous part of my system. He again seated himself, drew his butcher-knife from its greasy scabbard, examined its edge, as I would do that of a razor suspected dull, replaced it, and again taking his tomahawk from his back, filled the pipe of it with tobacco, and sent me expressive glances whenever our hostess chanced to have her back towards us.

Never until that moment had my senses been awakened to the danger which I now suspected to be about me. I returned glance for glance to my companion, and rested well assured that, whatever enemies I might have, he was not of their number.

I asked the woman for my watch, wound it up, and under pretense of wishing to see how the weather might probably be on the morrow, took up my gun, and walked out of the cabin. I slipped a ball into each barrel, scraped the edges of my flints, renewed the primings, and returning to the hut, gave a favorable account of my observations. I took a few bear-skins, made a pallet of them, and calling my faithful dog to my side, lay down, with my gun close to my body, and in a few minutes was, to all appearance, fast asleep.

A short time had elapsed, when some voices were heard, and from the corner of my eyes I saw two athletic youths making their entrance, bearing a dead stag on a pole. They disposed of their burden, and asking for whisky, helped themselves freely to it. Observing me and the wounded Indian, they asked who I was, and why the devil that rascal (meaning the Indian, who, they knew, understood not a word of English) was in the house. The mother —for so she proved to be, bade them speak less loudly, made mention of my watch, and took them to a corner, where a conversation took place, the purport of which it required little shrewdness in me to guess. I tapped my dog gently. He moved his tail, and with indescribable pleasure I saw his fine eyes alternately fixed on me and raised towards the trio in the corner. I felt that he perceived danger in my situation. The Indian exchanged a last glance with me.

The lads had eaten and drunk themselves into such condition, that I already looked upon them as hors de combat; and the frequent visits of the whisky bottle to the ugly mouth of their dam I hoped would soon reduce her to a like state. Judge of my astonishment, reader, when I saw this incarnate fiend take a large carving-knife, and go to the grindstone to whet its edge. I saw her pour the water on the turning machine, and watched her working away with the dangerous instrument, until the sweat covered every part of my body, in despite of my determination to defend myself to the last. Her task finished, she walked to her reeling sons, and said, *"There, that'll soon settle him! Boys, kill him, and then for the watch."*

I turned, cocked my gun-locks silently, touched my faithful companion, and lay ready to start up and shoot the first who might attempt my life. The moment was fast approaching, and that night might have been my last in this world, had not Providence made preparations for my rescue. All was ready. The infernal hag was advancing slowly, probably contemplating the best way of dispatching me, whilst her sons should be engaged with the Indian. I was several times on the eve of rising and shooting her on the spot:—but she was not to be punished thus. The door was suddenly opened, and there entered two stout travelers, each with a long rifle on his shoulder. I bounced up on my feet, and making them most heartily welcome, told them how well it was for me that they should have arrived at that moment. The tale was told in a minute. The drunken sons were secured, and the woman, in spite of her defense and vociferations, shared the same fate. The Indian fairly danced with joy, and gave us to understand that, as he could not sleep for pain, he would watch over us. You may suppose we slept much less than we talked. The two strangers gave me an account of their once having been themselves in a somewhat similar situation. Day came, fair and rosy, and with it the punishment of our captives.

They were now quite sobered. Their feet were unbound, but their arms were still securely tied. We marched them into the woods off the road, and having used them as Regulators were wont to use such delinquents, we set fire to the cabin, gave all the skins and implements to the young Indian warrior, and proceeded, well pleased towards the settlements.

During upwards of twenty-five years, when my wanderings extended to all parts of our country, this was the only time at which my life was in danger from my fellow creatures. Indeed, so little risk do travelers run in the United States, that no one born there ever dreams of any to be encountered on the road; and I can only account for this occurrence by supposing that the inhabitants of the cabin were not Americans.

Will you believe, reader, that not many miles from the place where this adventure happened, and where fifteen years ago, no habitation belonging to civilized man was expected, and very few ever seen, large roads are now laid out, cultivation has converted the woods into fertile fields, taverns have been erected, and much of what we Americans call comfort is to be met with. So fast does improvement proceed in our abundant and free country.

PRAIRIE FIRE!
Based on an Oral History Interview

My little sister and I were playing out in the yard, out by the well. My sister had some of them little corn husk dolls, maybe you've seen them?

Now I don't want you to get the wrong idea thinking a little boy would be playing with a doll. But back then we didn't have electronic gadgets, we didn't have electricity. We had to entertain ourselves, make our own fun. Anyhow, as I was playing with my sister and those little cornhusk dolls, our father came racing over the hill. I knew something was wrong by the way he was whipping that horse. Our father loved his horse sometimes we thought he loved his horse more than he loved his kids. He never whipped his horses, so I knew something was wrong.

Our father was yelling but we couldn't make out his words because he was too far away and the wind was whipping his voice around. But finally he was close enough we could understand. He said, "There's a fire coming, a prairie fire coming, run in the house and tell your ma!"

Back in those days we always did what our father told us, especially when he spoke in that tone of voice. So we ran in the house and my sister said, "Mom, mom there's a fire coming, a prairie fire coming!"

Now I almost forgot to tell you, we lived in a sod house. On the prairie there aren't many trees. Most people think sod houses are made out of grass, that's not exactly right. The truth is they use the roots and dirt. Most of the life of a prairie is underground. The grasses might be eight feet tall, but the roots go down 30 feet or more! The grass is shaved off. The top couple inches of grass and the bottom couple inches of roots are cut into bricks, like the brick house you might see around here. So our house was like a brick house except for one important difference: In the spring when it rains the grass will sprout and our house would turn green. In the summer, that grass would turn brown and dry. It was perfect kindling for a fire. So we ran in the house and I said, "Ma, ma there's a fire coming, a prairie fire coming."

Ma was kneading dough, baking bread, as she did most every day. When Ma heard those words her jaw dropped nearly to the floor. After she picked it up, she wiped the flour from her hands onto her apron. Peeling off her apron, she said, "Go round up your brothers and sisters, get all of the buckets you can find, and meet me outside by the well."

Well, I ran out behind the barn where my older brother was working in the garden. I ran back through the barn where my older sister was milking a cow. My sister dumped the bucket, we didn't want to cry over spilled milk… But we rounded up all of the buckets we could find and we met Ma by the well. By the time we arrived Ma had already pulled up the first bucket of water, she dumped it into my bucket. I handed it to my little sister, who handed it to my older brother, who handed it to my older sister, who took the bucket and dumped it on the house. We passed the empty bucket back to Ma.

Back and forth we were passing buckets and dumping them on the house. This makes sense right? When it was hot and dry we knew that one spark and this old soddy would burst into flames. This makes sense right?

While we were getting the house wet, pa started to do the strangest thing. I couldn't understand it, Pa took the horse out to the barn and he hitched up the plow.

I thought, summer is not plowing season, you plow the fields in the spring not the summer.

But Pa wasn't plowing the fields, he started plowing a circle around the house and the barn. Not once but twice, three, four, five times.

By now the house was good and wet so we turned our attention to the barn. Buckets going back and forth, full ones on the barn, empties back to Ma.

The barn was actually made out of wood. With what little lumber we had out here on the prairie we built the animals a nice home first because the barn was taller and needed the structural strength of wood. Ma said that the animals did live better than us - Pa did love his horse more than us, she teased.

We were dumping water onto the barn, that makes sense right? But then Pa moved the plow about 10 or 15 yards out and he started plowing bigger circles.

We were dumping bucket after bucket, buckets of water back and forth, full ones onto the barn and empties back to Ma. That makes sense right? Then I thought for sure that Pa had plum lost his mind. He went into the house with a shovel. He took a shovel of red hot coals...We always kept a fire going even in the heat of the summer for cooking and such. Pa took the red hot coals out to the front yard and he started a fire.

There was a prairie fire coming, why was he starting another one? But Pa knew what he was doing! Pa was burning the grass between the circles where he had plowed. He was making a fire break.

Good thing he did because it was just about then that we could smell the fire coming. Like some distant campfire, ribs bar-b-cueing on the grill!

It was just about then that we could feel the temperature rise. Within about 5 minutes the temperature climbed by 10 then 20 degrees. Maybe you know that on a hot summer day it can be 95 or 100 degrees, but on that day it felt like 105, 110, 120! It felt like your skin was going to boil and drip off the bone!

It was just about then that we could hear the fire coming. At first it sounded like a freight train but I know that the freight train hadn't made it that far west quite yet. Then it sounded like a dozen freight trains! Then it sounded like a tornado and then a dozen tornados. It was the loudest thing that I'd ever heard.

It was just about then that we could see the fire coming! We saw a wall of fire 30 feet high and a hundred miles wide. It came racing over the ridge. Pa explained later that because the fire sucks in the oxygen, it makes it own wind and sometimes it races across the prairie at 30-60 miles an hour!

As quick as it came, it was gone again.

But it rained sparks and ashes. Because Ma had taken the last bucket of water and dumped it on us kids, we were safe. Because the house and barn were good and wet, the sparks that fell on the house and barn did not catch Because Pa had made the fire break, it burned around not through our lives.

Come Sunday morning, when I heard the preacher talk about fire and brimstones falling from the sky I knew what he was talking about, because I had seen the fire falling from the sky! And Lord knows we went to church come Sunday to give thanks, because we survived. We survived the prairie fire because we had worked together. And I knew, if we could survive a prairie fire, we could survive anything!

29

COUGAR ON THE ROOF!
Based on Oral History

When I was little we used to walk two miles to school every day... uphill... both ways! Has your grandma or grandpa ever told you a story like this? If not, maybe we need to spend a little more time sitting with our grandparents collecting stories about what their life was like way back when they were little! The last story and this next one come from the oral tradition. I heard different versions of these stories sitting and listening to grandparents. And I will admit that since I have heard several stories like these, I have borrowed little pieces from here and there. Like an old family quilt, I stitched this story together from different scraps of colorful cloth. I am grateful to all of the grandmas and grandpas who have taken the time to share these stories.

When I was little we used to walk two miles to school every day. Most days it was like a parade! Because our house was the furthest from the settlement, as we walked along other boys and girls would join in and soon we were all marching along together... on a good day...

On a cold winter day, Ma would put a few old field stones in the fireplace the night before so they would get red hot. Those round granite rocks were left here by the glaciers ten thousand years ago. In the morning Ma would use a set of elk antlers or a pitch fork to pick up the glowing red rocks. She put them in the bottom of the sleigh by our feet. Those rocks would keep us warm as we rode to school. We were wrapped up in an old buffalo robe or horse hair blanket.

Over the river and through the woods to the one-room school we go! Jingle bells, jingle bells, all the way to school!

Come to think about it, that one horse open sleigh was our big yellow school bus. We would pick up the other kids along the way and soon a dozen of us would be piled into the sled! Once we got to school we would put the rocks on the pot belly stove so they would be hot when we rode home… on a good day…

But on the day I am remembering, just a few days before Christmas, there was a cold wind howling across the prairie. Pa had business to attend to in the next town over. He needed the sled so we had to walk to school, two miles, with snow up over our boots, and that cold wind sending shivers down our backs. B-r-r-r!

Then, when we got to the settlement the school marm said, *"Boys and girls, I got to send you home. That old pot belly stove will not keep this one-room school house warm enough. You will catch your death of a cold!"*

Now, how many of you like a snow day? Yeah… But we walked two miles for nothing? Two Miles FOR NOTHING!!!

Well, we looked around and decided that since all of our friends were there, we would make a day of it!

A few of the bigger boys and girls began making a snow ball, rolling and packing, rolling and packing, rolling and packing, until they had made the biggest snow ball you ever did see! While the big boys and girls were making a big snow ball, us middle-sized boys and girls made a middle-sized snow ball. And the little boys and girls made a little snow ball. But that snow man was so tall my older brother had to pick me up onto his shoulders to put the head up on top! It was the biggest snow man you ever did see!

One of the girls thought he looked kind of lonely so we made a snow woman, too. And a snow girl and a snow boy and a snow dog, and we even tried to make a snow cow, but it kept falling down! It was amazing what we could do when we all worked together!

Then one of the older girls, she was always in charge, she said, "Now everyone line up behind me, like follow the leader. Make sure you step in my foot prints so there are only one set of tracks." We followed her up onto the hillside. When she gave the signal, we all fell over onto our backs, moved our arms and legs just so... Then we were very careful to step in the same set of tracks as we walked down off the hill. More than a snow angel, with only one set of tracks, it looked like an entire choir of angels singing Ha-Lay-Lou-Ya to the Lord!

Then this boy got a devilish idea. He made a snow ball... and another one... and another... and another... and he let it fly. WHAAA! Ha Ha Ha! We had the best snow ball fight you ever you did see! But you know how it is when you get snow down the middle of your back? And you know that winter days are short, winter nights are long. We were coming up on the longest night of the year. That winter sun was heading towards the western sky. We knew we had better hurry home if we were going to get there before dark.

Now, I told you how walking to school was kind of like a parade; but walking home was always kind of lonely. One by one, two or three, boys and girls would disappear as we walked past their houses. Finally, the last mile, it was just my big brother, little sister and I.

As we were walking along I got this sneaking suspicion. Do you know the feeling like someone or something is watching you? Like eyes are burning holes in the back of your head. I turned around, but I didn't see anything suspicious. But that feeling that we were being followed would not go away!

I tugged my big brother on the sleeve. I told him what I was thinking. He said, *"Oh you read too many of them scary stories. It's just your imagination."*

I told him, *"My teacher said you can not read too much of anything as long as you are reading something!"*

And even though he said he did not believe me, I noticed, he kept looking over his shoulder like something or someone was following us… but whatever it was… we didn't see it… until after we got home…

When we got home, Pa wasn't there yet. Ma said he might spend the night in town and come home tomorrow.

Now, whenever we got home we had chores to do. We had one rule in our house: we could not eat until all of the animals have been fed. So every morning it was hay to the cows, slop to the pigs, scratch to the chickens, we would gather the eggs and then we could eat breakfast. And every evening, it was the same routine before we could eat supper.

Ma had made a pot of elk stew, cooked over the fire, simmering all day. It always tastes better that way. She also made ash cakes or Johnny cakes. Do you like pancakes? These are kind of like pancakes, but they are made out of corn meal. They are cooked on a hot rock in the fire, that's why they call them ash cakes. You scrape off the ashes and dunk them in your stew, m-m-m-m, nothing ever tasted so good!

In those days we didn't have electricity, so after it got dark we went to bed. We lived in a little one room cabin out on the prairie. We were near a timber so we had a log cabin, but we had a thatch roof, you know… like they have over in Ireland. Pa took big bundles of tall prairie grasses and tied them together. He then laid them over the roof, like shingles, to help shed the rain and the snow and to keep the house warm. Ma and Pa's bed was in one corner. My little sister had a trundle bed that we would tuck under Ma's bed during the day.

My brother and I slept in the loft, like a shelf, above the fireplace, so we were always warm on a cold winter night. We climbed the ladder to the loft. Ma tucked us in and told us a bed time story. You are never too old for a good story. But just as Ma was finishing the story we heard it... whatever it was... it was up on the roof...

It started scratching and pawing and digging, scratching and pawing and digging, right above my bed, dirt falling down on my head. Ma did not know know what to do! Pa had taken the rifle. But Ma was a resourceful woman. She climbed down and picked up the poker, you know, the metal pole you use to stir the fire. She put it in the fire, so it was getting red hot! Whatever was up on the roof, it kept scratching and pawing and digging. Eventually a huge paw came down through the thatch. It was a cougar!

Now some folks call them Mountain Lions, but we don't have any mountains out on the prairie, so we called them cougars, or panthers. And there it was trying to dig down through our roof! By now the poker was good and hot! Ma grabbed the poker and let that cougar have it! ROAR! It screamed, pulled back its paw and leapt away. But it did not run away! It started digging another hole in the roof!

Ma put the poker back in the fire. Now the first time it took that cougar maybe five minutes to make that first hole, but with a bum paw it took longer the second time. Plenty of time for the poker to get red hot! As soon as that paw came down through the roof, ROAR! Ma let him have it! All night long!

Somewhere in the middle of the night I could not keep my eyes open. But every time I started to fall asleep, ROAR! Ma let that cougar have it! All night long! Ma never went to sleep, because, well, you know about the love of a mother for her children!

34

Somewhere early in the morning, as we saw the first fingers of light creeping over the horizon, we saw someone else coming over the hill. It was Pa! He stopped the sleigh. He reached in behind the bench seat and grabbed his rifle. He stood up in the sleigh. He took careful aim. And KABLAM! He missed! The cougar jumped down and ran off in the opposite direction. Pa came riding up to the house as fast as that horse could go! Pa burst into the cabin. He counted heads. When he saw that all of us were still alive and Ma was still holding the poker, he gave Ma a great big hug, because, well, she saved our lives!

Then Pa went out and he tracked that cougar. He said at first it was easy to follow the tracks with the blood and all, but running across the snow the bleeding stopped. Then it ran out onto the river where the ice was smooth as glass. The tracks disappeared. Some folks call the cougar the ghost of the prairie, the way its tawny brown fur blends in so well with the tawny brown prairie grasses, perfect camouflage.

So Pa turned around and followed the cougar back from whence he had come. Pa said my sneaking suspicion was correct! That cougar had followed us home from school! Pa said that when there were a number of boys and girls, it stayed off in the tall prairie grasses. As more and more children disappeared, the cougar became more brave. The last mile there were cougar tracks on top of our tracks!

Pa said he noticed something else, too. See, Pa could read tracks the way some folks read a book. That cougar had a strange limp, even before he met Ma. It was like he was lame or something, because the tracks were not real evenly spaced. Pa figured because that cougar was lame, he was desperate. He could not catch a deer. That's why he followed us home. And I do not know about you, but I cannot run as fast as a deer. That cougar must have thought we would be an easy catch, but he had not figured on Ma. Because that cougar was starving he would not give up.

But Ma, she saved our lives, because, well, you know about the love of a mother for her children!

THE SEED
Four Seasons On The Prairie

A teardrop-shaped seedpod cracks open in the wind. The milkweed scatters its seed. Parachutes catch the breeze. Some seeds fall close by. Others are carried a mile or more away. As they settle on the earth, they are covered in blankets of red, orange, yellow, and brown. Autumn leaves bury the seeds.

Honk, honk, honk. In long V's the Canada geese fly south for the winter. When they fly together, the front of the V formation slices the air to make flying easier for those coming behind. The lead goose also creates a wave of air with the flapping of its wings. This wave of air, or current, helps to lift and lower the wings of the geese behind. So the geese at the back of the V are pulled along on currents of air by the geese in the front of the line. When the lead goose grows tired, it slips back to rest, and another goose takes the lead. Taking turns all the way, the geese make their way south. By day, they follow landmarks and are guided by the angle of the sun. By night, they are guided by the moon and stars.

In the autumn, monarch butterflies gather to form huge clouds of orange and black. The clouds grow and grow as more butterflies join them, and then the clouds merge into long, trailing rivers of fluttering wings. Together these winged creatures fly south for the winter. When they rest on a tree, the tree is transformed into a living mosaic of orange and black, a dazzling feast for the eyes. These fragile creatures fly more than 1,000 miles to the fir forests of central Mexico.

A huge black bear, full of the fruits of summer, fat from the fall harvest of nuts, begins looking for a place to sleep. In the open prairie there are few caves. Maybe the bear curls up under a cluster of oaks or climbs down a creek bank, where she finds a cave carved by the moving water. Or maybe, where a great burr oak has fallen, the pulled up root ball creates a small cave where the bear can bury herself in oak leaves.

The frog burrows in the mud at the bottom of a pond. Its body slows down. It stops breathing. Its heart almost stops beating. This is true hibernation. If you were to find a frog in the middle of winter, you would think it was dead. If you held it in your hands, the heat from your hands would warm the frog and it would seem to come to life, slowly

After the work of a season is done, after the acorns have fallen, the leaves of the oak change color. They seem to catch fire as they become brilliant red, bright orange, bronze, and yellow. The winds blow, and the oak tree drops its leaves.

The fox squirrel gathers acorns. It eats its fill and buries the rest of the nuts in the ground. All through the autumn the squirrel eats as many nuts as it can, and puts some aside for winter when food is hard to find. The squirrel also gathers the falling leaves and makes a nest in the crotch of the tree. A thick layer of oak leaves keeps it warm when the cold winds blow.

Winter

The north winds howl and snow begins to fall. The seeds of the milkweed are buried in a blanket of white. They lie through the long winter, waiting for spring.

As the snow falls on the milkweed, the geese are having a party under the warm Mexican sun.

Like true kings and queens, the monarch butterflies winter in the mountains of Mexico. They are somewhat dormant while the northern lands brace for another storm.

As the snow falls, as the pond turns to ice, the frog hibernates safely, snugly, under the mud.

In her cave or snug spot, the bear enters a deep sleep. Bears do not enter a complete hibernation: they stir occasionally in the depths of winter. In the second week of January, bears throughout this land awake to give birth. Cubs are born. The mother licks them clean and goes back to sleep.

You may think that great big bears would have great big babies, but a bear cub could fit in the palm of your hand. The newborn cubs crawl up their mother's belly and drink her milk. The fruits of summer that were converted to fat are once more transformed, this time into mother's milk. Throughout the winter, while their mother is sleeping, the cubs drink and sleep, sleep and drink.

Through the winter the oak tree stands dormant. Its branches are laden with snow and rattled by the winds. But if you look closely at an oak in winter, if you look 10 times more closely at the branches, you will see the tips of buds, and inside the buds you will find tiny leaves formed in the fall, waiting for spring.

The fox squirrel does not hibernate. When the weather is very cold, the squirrel may sleep for five or six days. Could you imagine sleeping for five or six days? When the fox squirrel wakes up, it has one thing on its mind: food!

Do you think squirrels can remember where they buried all of their acorns? Do you think squirrels can even remember where they buried some of those acorns? Not at all. So how do they find their nuts? They use their sense of smell. A squirrel can smell through six inches of snow, three inches of leaves, and three inches of dirt—up to one foot of matter—to find an acorn. On the coldest days, the squirrel may add more leaves to its nest before curling up for another long sleep.

Waking, eating, sleeping. Over and over the squirrel wakes, sniffs around, digs up hidden treasures, eats, and goes back to sleep, waiting for the warm breath of spring.

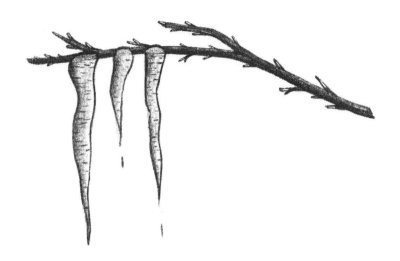

Spring

A warm southeastern breeze begins to blow, and the snow begins to melt. Spring rains start to fall. The milkweed seed swells, soaking in the moisture. A tiny sprout pushes down, deep down, into the Earth. The roots begin to reach out, drinking in moisture and minerals. The leaves push up through the soil, through the clutter of dried stalks and old leaves, reaching for the warmth and light of the sun. Throughout the spring the little plant stretches up toward the sun.

As the days grow longer and the sun returns to this land, so do the geese. Have you heard the geese heralding the return of spring? Honk, honk, honk. Canada geese, which mate for life, build a nest. The female lays eggs, and both mother and father take turns keeping them warm. Both mother and father take turns feeding their young and protecting them from the dangers of this world.

The monarch butterflies also return north. Though one monarch makes the journey south, it takes three or four generations to make the trip north. In early March the butterflies that flew south begin the journey north. When the milkweed of the southern states begin to sprout, these butterflies stop to lay eggs. Their offspring hatch, eat milkweed leaves, metamorphose into adults, and continue the journey north. When the milkweed of the central states begin to sprout, these butterflies stop to lay eggs. These grandchildren hatch, eat milkweed leaves, metamorphose into adults, and continue the journey north. It is the great-grandchildren of the butterflies that headed south who return to the northern prairie in the late spring, just as the milkweed unfurl their leaves. The monarchs lay their eggs on the young milkweed leaves. The eggs hatch. The young caterpillars eat the leaves. As they eat they grow. As they grow they shed their skin. They eat, they grow, and they shed.

Milkweed leaves are poisonous to most creatures, but the monarch caterpillar is immune. In fact, they use the poison to their advantage! After it eats the milkweed, the plant's poison is inside the monarch caterpillar (and later the butterfly). If a creature ate the monarch it would also eat the poison. The creature would become very sick and vomit, it does not usually die. Any creature that survives would never eat another monarch caterpillar or butterfly!

The bears come out of their den and look for food. The mother has eaten nothing for three months or more. She begins to teach her cubs what to eat, how to hunt and gather. What do you think bears eat? If you said meat, you might be surprised. Black bears usually eat fruits, roots, nuts, and insects. Occasionally they might catch a mouse or chipmunk. Or, if they find a fresh carcass, they might eat some meat. As omnivores they will eat anything that tastes good, but black bears eat mostly plant material.

With the spring thaw the frog begins to stir. It swims to the top of the pond and gulps its first breath as life begins anew! When you hear the frogs singing, you know that spring is truly here.

The frogs are singing to find a mate. The female exudes a string of slimy eggs that the male then fertilizes. This clump of jelly, filled with tiny black dots, hides in the murky water.

If you looked closely at those tiny black dots, 100 times more closely, you would see the stages of evolution before your very eyes. Inside one egg, from a single cell, split in two and split again, comes 4 cells, 8 cells, 16, 32 . . . 64 . . . 128 . . . 1,012 . . . 16,000 . . . 384,000. More than 1 million cells form from those first 2 cells! Cells specialize, change into muscles, skin, gills, nerves. A brain forms.

You went through these same changes inside your mother's womb. You were once an egg. Then you looked like a worm. Then you grew gills, a spine, a brain. Your gills and tail disappeared. You kept growing and changing until you became more fully human.

The tadpole forms inside the egg. When it is ready it breaks out of the slimy gelatin and begins to swim around.

As the world bursts into life, the sap rises in the ancient oak. Buds form and flowers burst forth. Oak flowers are like human flowers: the male flower and female flower are separate. That's unusual for a flower. If you cut open a tulip, you will find the pistil (that's the female part) and the stamen (the male part) together in the same blossom. Most flowers are like that. It makes it easier for them to reproduce. But with oak flowers, the male part and the female part are separate. So how do oak flowers get together? They use the wind. The wind carries the pollen from the male flower to the female flower. The pollen fertilizes the ovule (egg), and an acorn gets its start in life.

All that new life is tempting for a starving squirrel. When the weather begins to warm up, the squirrel comes out of its deep sleep. It begins to eat the buds of trees, the eggs of birds, and baby birds. The squirrel cleans out her nest to make room for her own babies, which she must protect from larger enemies. Baby squirrels are so small you could hold several in one hand. They are blind and helpless at birth, completely dependent on their parents. Mother's milk and a mother's care help them to grow into frolicking pups.

Summer

A southern breeze blows, and spring spins into summer. The goslings lose their fuzz and begin to grow flight feathers. The adults molt, dropping their old feathers so they can grow new ones. The young geese learn to fly and the old geese prepare for their long flight back to their winter home.

The hot sun showers its light upon the young milkweed. The leaves soak up the sunlight and convert it to food; soon, the plant produces flowers. Tiny buds push up and open, releasing their rich fragrance, attracting butterflies and bees—and humans.

A monarch butterfly visits the pink-and-white blossom to sip the sweet nectar, an enticing treat. The butterfly has pollen on its feet from other flowers it has visited. Look closely at its feet, 1,000 times more closely, and you will see tiny grains of pollen like cockleburs with Velcro grippers. They grab onto the pistil, the female part of the flower, and burrow deep into its base. The pollen joins with the ovary and a tiny seed is made.

Before the butterfly leaves, its feet slip into a little trap on the side of the flower. There it picks up more pollen to take to the next milkweed. The butterfly gets the sweet, sticky nectar as a reward for performing this all-important task of pollination.

This adult butterfly may also lay tiny eggs on the underside of the milkweed's leaves. In about 5 days the eggs will hatch into tiny black, yellow, and white caterpillars. Like generations before, the caterpillar eats, grows, and sheds. It will crack its old skin and crawl out, shedding 5 times before it is ready for metamorphosis.

When it is ready, it attaches its back end to a twig and hangs upside down. It does not spin a protective cocoon; instead it splits its skin and rolls it back, exposing a wriggling emerald green sack known as a chrysalis. Using parts of its old self, it dissolves what it used to be to make itself new! After several days, the walls of the chrysalis become transparent. If you look closely you can see the crumpled black and orange wings. The chrysalis cracks open, and the new adult emerges. It pumps fluid into its wings and flies away to repeat the cycle. Three or four generations of butterflies live and die in a prairie summer.

All summer long, the bears forage for food. They eat strawberries in the early summer; blackberries in the middle of summer; blueberries in late summer; and wild grapes, plums, acorns, and hickory nuts in the early autumn. They eat ants from earthen mounds and termites from infested logs whenever they can find them.

Through the warm summer the frog continues to evolve. The tadpole, a fishlike swimmer, sprouts legs. Its tail dissolves and disappears. The frog begins to breathe air and leaps about upon the land. Like a sticky whip, its long tongue snatches insects from the air.

The leaves of the oak tree make food to feed the tree and to feed its acorns. Like food factories, the leaves convert the energy of sunlight into nutrients the tree can use. The little acorns grow plumper and plumper. By late summer, they are fat and brown, full of the nutrients they need to start another small oak—or feed a squirrel.

Scurrying from branch to branch, leaping from tree to tree, playing tag as they race around the trunk, the young squirrels race through summer. Their meals depend on the cycle of seeds, fruits, and nuts. Maple, cherry, mulberry, ash, crabapple, oak, hickory, and walnut—each of these trees will feed the young squirrels in turn. And, the young squirrels help to disperse the seeds.

The leaves of the milkweed continue to harvest the sunlight and convert it to food. The seed pod is formed. The seeds continue to grow, and a parachute begins to form. Each seed is given the food it needs to begin life.

Autumn

Autumn winds blow down from the northwest.

Young frogs swim to the bottom of the pond and burrow under the mud.

The bears begin looking for a place to sleep. During their first winter, the nearly grown cubs will sleep with their mother. Next winter they will have to find a place of their own.

Leaves fall. The days grow shorter, signaling the geese it's time to head south. They fly day and night in long V's, filling the air with their cries. Honk, honk, honk. They herald the return of winter.

The monarch butterflies gather in clouds of orange and black for the long migration south.

The fall harvest fattens young squirrels as they prepare for winter. A teardrop-shaped seedpod cracks open in the wind. The milkweed scatters its seed. Parachutes catch the breeze. Some seeds fall close by. Others are carried a mile or more away. As they settle on the Earth, they are covered in blankets of red, orange, yellow, and brown. Autumn leaves bury the seeds.

And this story begins again!

THE BLUE CRAWFISH
A Wildlife Adventure

The earliest settlers in Illinois were sometimes called suckers. Illinois was known as 'The Sucker State' because of the abundance of crawdad holes. If you were out on a hot dry day, they say that you could put your lips on such a hole and if you sucked hard enough you could get water. I am not sure if this is true, but that is what they say. We do know that the crawfish tunnel does go down to the water table, the aquifer. As you wander across the prairies and lawns of Illinois today, if you watch carefully down at your feet you might avoid stumbling over the chimney of a beautiful blue terrestrial crawfish.

Chimney really is the perfect word for these well designed, expertly constructed entrances, (or exits), to the underground labyrinths of the blue crawfish. Underground they dig up a ball of dirt. As they roll the mud up out of their tunnel the ball becomes a smooth sphere. The crawfish piles the balls up into a cylindrical chimney. This chimney helps to keep water out of the tunnel. And when the air is hot and dry during a drought they can cap their chimney to keep moisture in the tunnel. Even though these crayfish are acting 'terrestrial' they need their gills to stay moist so they can breath. And if you were a crayfish with the right senses you might notice that chimneys also have chemical cues that help young crayfish find safe places to burrow near their own species.

These tunnels aerate the prairie allowing prairie roots to breath. They allow drainage for the inundating summer cloudbursts. They provide homes for countless beetles, spiders, snakes and other squatters in the subterranean world of the prairie. Burrows can be anywhere from 3-15 feet deep. They're also great for nutrient cycling because crayfish eat and poop, they decompose plant and animal matter, providing finer forms of nutrients for plants and insects. Their burrowing helps pull these nutrients to the surface. Most of the biomass, the life of a prairie, is actually underground.

Let's go into that world!

Imagine shrinking down to the size of a crawdad. Imagine being 5 to 10 centimeters long. Imagine growing a hard blue shiny exoskeleton, a beautiful blue shell, large claws in front and six smaller pinchers on each of the first three pairs of your eight crab-like legs. Because the first two claws count as legs, you actually have ten legs. Imagine having a fin like tail, a tail like a mermaid, only it is stiff. Stretch and crawl, get used to this new outer shell and crawling with 10 legs. Peek out through retractable eyes and feel your way along with thin sensitive antennae.

As the crawfish crawls down the tunnel the darkness gradually becomes complete. The eyes retract for protection and the antennae become the primary sense organ. The crawfish senses every subtle vibration and feels the edges of the tunnel as it curves and slopes slowly down deeper and deeper into the ground.

These tunnels split and curve into several directions; this allows the crawfish an opportunity to hunt a wider range of soil for grubs, beetles, worms, and other living morsels.

The blue crawfish pauses. It feels vibrations, movement in one of its tunnels. It races along, lunging at an earthworm. The worm flops completely into the tunnel. Sensing the crawfish approaching, the worm begins searching for a way out. It finds its hole and immediately begins to retreat, hoping to pass through the tunnel unnoticed.

Just as the worm is about to disappear into its hole, the crawfish snatches the worm's tail, cutting it in half. Half of the worm crawls away leaving a trail of blood. The other half is wriggling in the crawfish's claws. With the smaller pinchers on its feet it pulls what's left into its mouth and begins to eat. Half of a worm is still a good catch! The half that got away will grow a new tail and might be there as a meal for another day.

Above ground a gentle rain begins to fall. Gradually, it turns into a torrent. Big black clouds open up and pour buckets of rain onto the prairie. Lightening flashes! Thunder roars! The chimney protects the tunnel from a light rain, but as golf-ball-sized pieces of hail pummel the ground the chimney collapses. Surface water begins pouring into the crawfish hole. The ground is already saturated from a wet spring so it doesn't take long for the soil to become completely soaked.

The tunnels begin to fill with water and the crawfish is faced with a dilemma. It can stay under water for some time and breathe through its gills. But a soaking rain means that much of its food is heading out onto unprotected ground. The ground is super-saturated with water. Any creature underground without gills would drown. A fine feast awaits the crayfish up above, but there is also the threat of becoming someone else's dinner.

As the tunnel fills with water, the blue crawfish catches the bubbles rising to the top and gets a free lift towards the surface. It cautiously approaches the exit to its tunnel. Its senses tell it that it is getting dark, or is it just the dark clouds? Timidly, it crawls out of its tunnel and onto the ground. The tall grass prairie offers some protection. There are worms and grubs squirming about everywhere! The blue crawfish snatches a worm and devours it. It quickly makes a meal of several other small insects and grubs. In this feeding frenzy it pays less and less attention to what is going on around it.

The rain stops and the sun peeks out from behind the clouds as it descends. A prairie chicken, who is also gorging on the worms washed up by the rain, sees the blue crawfish. The chicken struts over and pecks at the crayfish. The first blow hits the middle of the hard back shell. The prairie chicken's beak bounces off, but before the crawfish can get away, the chicken rears back for another peck. This time it grabs one of the thin spidery legs and picks the crayfish up into the air. Shaking its head, the prairie chicken snaps off the leg, tossing the crawfish several feet. It scoots backwards using its powerful tail. It bounces off a few ice cubes, melting hail, trying desperately to get away from the prairie chicken. The prairie chicken with a quick flap of her wings and three leaps pounces on it again.

At the last possible second, the blue crawfish stumbles into a hole and slips away. The prairie chicken squawks a few times and pecks at the ground, but quickly gives up and resumes eating the easier catch, worms and insects who do not put up a fight. Safely underground, the blue crawfish rests. Injured, but alive, the next time the crawfish molts it will actually grow a new leg! The prairie chicken doesn't win today!!

After a few hours, when it is fully dark, the crawfish rebuilds its chimney. Scooping a small ball of dirt, it carefully rolls it up, up, up out of his tunnel. One ball, then another, until eventually twenty or more balls of mud are excavated. On the surface, the balls are stacked into neat cylindrical piles. The blue crawfish works under the cover of darkness. In one night the chimney has been rebuilt and a new tunnel has been excavated.

So the next time you are walking through a tall grass prairie or even in your own backyard and you see a carefully constructed mud chimney, pause for a moment and allow your imagination to wander down into the subterranean world of the prairie, through the thick tangle of roots and rhizomes, through the rich soil and glacial rocks, into the adventurous world of the blue crawfish.

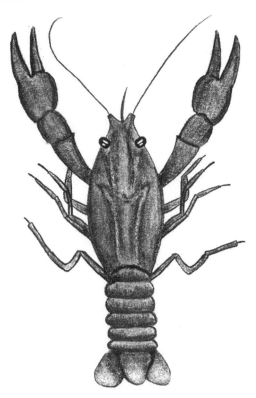

ONE TRUE LOVE, A WISE FOOL, AND AN
OLD ROMANTIC
Three Folktales About Flowers Adapted From the Lakota

One True Love - The Spiderwort

I cannot pick a favorite flower… but if the proper pressure were asserted I can fearlessly say the spiderwort is in the top ten. It is a relative of the common day lily. With long grass like leaves, about three feet tall, it has more than a dozen buds on each slender stalk. One flower opens on each plant every day for several weeks in May and June. In a large clump of these plants there could be a hundred fresh flowers every morning. The flower is a soft blue with three triangular petals. Sometimes it has a pink, purple, or even a pale, almost whitish hue. There are 75 species including the Virginia Spiderwort, Ohio Spiderwort and the Hairy Spiderwort. It blooms from the prairies of Canada to the pampas of Argentina.

Every part of the plant is edible. The leaves and flowers can be tossed into salads and if you chew the leaves and place them on a wound as a poultice, like a band-aid, it is healing. It is even good for hemorrhoids! If you plant a few in your garden they are sure to spread, hopefully into your neighbors' yards so everyone is blessed with this beautiful flower.

Once, while I was driving along an old country road, parallel with an even older railroad track, I noticed they were widening the roadway. They were destroying the native prairie that followed the railroad grade. That was the real crime. But right now, before God and Country, I will publicly admit that I may have broken the law. With true love as my motivation, I stopped my car, grabbed a shovel and a few bags, and I dug up several species of prairie plants that were about to be paved over. The one that thrived and has since been transplanted into several of my home gardens was a rare species of spiderwort.

I do love the spiderwort. I love the mildly fragrant flowers. I love its hardy nature. I love that the early summer bees love it. I love that it spreads its love readily around my garden.

According to Melvin R. Gilmore's historic collection of Plains Indians Folklore, Prairie Smoke, it seems I am not the only one who loves this plant. According to the Lakota, when a young man is in love and he comes across a large clump of the spiderwort flowers blooming on the prairie he will sit next to these flowers. He will admire their beauty. And then he will sing to them. He will make up a song that uses the flower's beauty as a symbol of the beauty of his one true love. Gilmore's translation of the traditional Dakota song goes something like this:

> Tiny, handsome flower
> Petals delicate like wings
> Modest, yet gorgeous
> My love for thee I sing

Maybe the next time you see these beautiful triangular shaped little blue flowers you can sing a song to your true love. With permission, collect some seeds or dig a few roots and plant them in your garden. Share the love with your neighbors and friends!

A Wise Fool - The Sunflower

Among the First Nations People the clown is the wise fool, Heya-hoka! They will often make a fool of themself to highlight the foolish choices we make. Sometimes their foolish pantomime will make us laugh! Ha, Ha, Ha, Ha! And sometimes their antics cause us to drop our heads, embarrassed, as we rethink the choices we have made. They challenge us to make better choices, with their absolutely hilarious performances.

Early one morning a group of young men were riding their ponies across the prairie. The night before they had performed their dances. They had painted their faces as ferocious warriors. They had sharpened their spears and counted their arrows, ready for battle against a foe who deserved to die!

As these warriors made their way through the tall grass prairie, moving silently so their foe did not know they were there, they heard a strange song. A ridiculous song? Was this Heya-hoka? At first they snickered. A clown singing a silly song! Ha, ha, ha, ha! But their smiles turned to clenched teeth. Was this song about them? Were they about to die? Kill or be killed? For what? For pride...

As the sunlight rose behind them, they saw a person moving through the tall grass. Was it human? It was dressed in rags, green plumage, like leaves. It danced in the early morning breeze. Its face was painted with large yellow circles. It stared directly into the rising sun. As the morning fog disappeared they saw more clearly. It shuffled. It stopped. As the sun rose its face followed the path of the sun across the sky.

Look into the light! Do not be afraid. Face the truth.

Watch the young sunflower as it tracks the sun across the sky. In the morning it faces east. At mid-day it faces south. Early evening comes and it watches the sun going down. And yet at dawn it is facing east once more.

The compass plant, prairie dock, and Maximillian's sunflower still track the sun in their youth, and they face the east in their final days. May we too learn to face the light, face the truth, and in our final days know the sun alway rises in the east.

An Old Romantic - Prairie Smoke

A friend of mine, knowing my affection for the prairie smoke flower, recently brought me a flat of a dozen flowers to plant in my prairie. In late winter I keep watch because they are the first flowers to bloom in the prairie, sometimes blooming while a late snow gently falls. Their flower heads look like mine, wispy gray hair, hard to call it a flower at all, but it has such simple beauty. Like a slow burning fire with the occasional wisp of smoke, hence the name prairie smoke.

It is fire resistant. And it blooms just after the time we light the fires to burn away the duff, the remnants of last years prairie grasses, so we can turn all of that carbon into ash, into fertilizer, so the prairie blooms more brightly in the future.

Can you imagine an old man, like me, out walking across a broad expanse of wild prairie. There are undulating hills, swaths of tall grasses and buffalo wallows where the grasses are gone and bare earth is visible. There are burr oak growing in the distance and a flock of snow geese cackling faintly even further away. But if you look down, there is a small patch of prairie smoke flowers. Prairie smokes' faint gray wisps fluttering in the breeze blowing along the ground.

Can you imagine an old man kneeling here? Offering an affectionate prayer to the flowers yet to bloom... I offer a prayer to the flowers you will plant. I offer blessings to the flower children who will bloom a hundred years after I am gone. I am remembering the prairie flowers I have known and wishing you might know their offspring, the prairie flowers of the next seven generations. May your children know the prairies of the future rooted in the plantings of the past.

May each of us learn the names of flowers yet to bloom. May we fall in love with the lowliest blossoms. May we live long enough to become the elders who look back at the seeds we have planted and still have hope for the romantic love of what might yet still be.

A WILD LIFE:
Scientific Research and Short Story Form

You can be a wild life researcher! In your neighborhood, local park, or maybe even in your backyard, are hundreds of wild animals living amazing, dangerous and curious lives that we as humans know very little about. Much like the Blue Crayfish that lives underground in my neighborhood. When you carefully observe these animals in their home they will reveal to you their habits and adventures. Use this form to organize your research and outline your story.

I. CHARACTER - The first step is to chose an animal. It should be one that you can easily observe most any day. There are many possibilities: a bird at your feeder, an ant in your backyard, a butterfly in your backyard prairie, a squirrel in a park nearby.

Draw its picture!

My animal is a _____.

Write a detailed description of what your animal looks like, how it moves, what it does, and any other interesting characteristics:

_____
_____
_____
_____
_____
_____

II. SETTING - The second step is to spend some time in the animal's environment or HABITAT. Take a journal and jot down some notes about its home. What types of plants and animals share its neighborhood? Is there a creek or river, any unusual rock or landforms nearby? Write a detailed description of your animal's NICHE or home:

_____
_____
_____
_____
_____
_____

III. PLOT - Let the research begin! Schedule regular times to sit quietly and unobtrusively in the animal's home and watch it very carefully. Ask yourself questions like: What does it eat? What might eat it? Where will it hide? Where does it sleep? What do you think it might do in bad weather? Does it have babies? What materials does it use to build its home?

Make up some questions of your own and then observe your animal for answers. The basic question is: How does this animal interact with its environment? Note everything that your animal does and then make an educated guess or hypothesis about what you think it will do next or why it did what it did. Watch carefully to see if your guess was accurate. Observe your animal at least fifteen minutes a day for seven days. Be careful not to disturb its daily habits. Always take careful notes, recording the time, the date, the weather and any other important information. You may also wish to supplement your observations with information from the library.

_____
_____
_____
_____
_____
_____

IV. THE STORY - Use the notes from your journal to write an exciting story about your animal! You may wish to begin with a description of the setting or character, plunge into a problem the animal faces, build tension, and then tell us how the animal resolves the problem. Good Luck! When you finish the story send me a copy and/or a video of you performing the story and I may use it on our Fox Tales International Youtube channel.

A Prairie Transect

A transect is basically a long line. In a scientific sense it is a long line along which you collect data. Collecting data along a transect gives you a good sample of the big picture. A prairie transect can give you a sense of the health and diversity of the prairie. If you do two transects, one north to south and another east to west across a park you can get a good picture of the health and diversity of a park. Your transect could be 10 meters long or 10 miles long. One prairie botanist, Kelly Kindscher, walked a 1000 mile transect across a long stretch of prairie from the mountains of the west to the forests of the east. He not only noted the names of plants and how the plant community changed from short grass to tall grass prairie, he collected data about edible and medicinal prairie plants!

What you need:
- A piece of string 10 meters long, (about ten yards or 30 feet long)
- A clip-board and pencil
- Books: field guides to prairie plants, insects, birds, and animal tracks &/or access to i-naturalist and on-line field guides on a tablet or smart phone

The basic idea is for you to do a simple comparison of a mowed lawn to a wild piece of prairie near your home. Which one do you think is more diverse? Which one has more species of plants and animals? What questions do you have about the two? How might they be alike or different?

First, divide your paper into two columns, draw a line down the middle of the page then title one column Mowed Lawn and the other Prairie. Next make a few predictions about what you think you might find in each site. Write down your lists on the clipboard. Write down any additional questions you might have.

Go outside!

Use your piece of string to make a straight line across a mowed lawn; it could be your yard or a local park. Slowly walk along that line and make a list of all of the creatures you see. Use the field guides &/or i-Naturalist to help you identify plants and animals you are not familiar with. Crawling along look for different types of plants and insects. Look up now and then to see if any birds fly over. Think about your line being a long rectangle one meter wide, about as wide as your arms stretch to each side of the string. If you see animal tracks or scat, (poop), or any clear sign that an animal was recently there you can add that animal to your list.

When you are done with your first transect go over your notes and organize them into categories. How many plants? What kinds? How many animals: birds; insects; and so on.

Next move your string to a wild prairie. If you can find an unplowed virgin prairie all the better. A restored prairie is good, but make sure it isn't just an un-mowed pasture or hayfield. Make a straight line across the prairie with your string. Again, think of it as a long, thin rectangle as wide as your arms, about a meter wide. Walk slowly along your string and list all of the plants and animals you can find. This transect will take a little longer and you will need to spend more time in your field guides identifying plants and insects. Look up more often for birds and flying bugs. Look closely for scat and tracks.

When you are done with your second transect go over your notes and organize them into categories. How many plants? What kinds? How many animals: birds; insects; and so on.
Now compare the two lists. What does the data tell you? What conclusions do you draw from the information? What additional questions arise?

You can use the data you collect to write your own story about an individual animal like The Blue Crayfish or a seasonal story like The Seed.

Write Your Own Story about Four Seasons on the Prairie

After reading "The Seed," fill in the chart below. First, list all of the characters in the column on the left. Then fill in the rows with information about what each character does in each season.

Use events described in the story, or use other events that you know about that are not in the story.

Using the chart, pick one character and write about what that character does in each season. OR pick one season and write about what all the characters do during that season. Hint: If you choose a character to write about, look across the chart at what you have written about that character in each of the four seasons. If you choose a season to write about, go down the column to find out what each of the characters does in that season. The short phrases you write in each box could also be used to write a poem.

Characters	AUTUMN	WINTER	SPRING	SUMMER

RESTORING PRAIRIES: One Yard at a Time

Use the grid on the next page to draw your yard and to plan your butterfly garden.

You can help restore a small piece of the prairie by planting native wildflowers in your home garden. These flowers can attract many beautiful species of butterflies, bees, and hummingbirds to your backyard. Draw a grid of your yard and map out a plan choosing a sunny area. As you are planning, think about the Rule of 9. Pick 9 flowers that each bloom at a different time: three spring, three summer, three fall. This way the bees and butterflies will always have nectar available to them. Take your plans to a local nursery that specializes in native wildflowers. Have them review your plans, give you advice, or help you acquire the correct plants or seeds for your area. Prepare the soil by plowing, tilling, or simply digging up the grass and turning it under. Many prairie plants grow in poor soil but if the plants or seeds you choose require additional nutrition you might need to add organic matter, sand, or lime to your soil. Butterflies prefer flowers with bright colors like purple, yellow, orange, and red, as well as flowers that produce a lot of nectar. It is also important to choose a variety of plants that caterpillars like to eat, (host plants), and to include flowers that continually bloom, spring through fall, to provide a constant food supply. After planting your flowers you can add a few prairie grasses for contrast and then look forward to the beautiful creatures that will visit your garden for years to come.

ABOUT THE STORIES & THEIR SOURCES:

- "A Prairie Fire" is from my book <u>Song of the Red Fox</u>, (Fox Tales International 2003).
- "The Woman Who Lived with the Wolves" is a traditional Lakota Story.
- "Buffalo Brothers" is from the book <u>Stories of the Sioux</u> by Luther Standing Bear, The University of Nebraska Press, used with permission.
- "The Prairie Dog and The Rain" is from Myths and Tales of the Jicarilla Apache Indians, By Morris Edward Opler, 1907.
- "The Prairie" by John James Audubon is one of 50 short stories he published in the 1830's as part of his monumental <u>The Birds of</u>
- <u>North America</u>.
- "Prairie Fire!" is based on a dozen oral history pieces I collected from eye-witnesses including my wife's grandmother Ruby Thrush. First published in my book <u>Content Area Reading, Writing, and Storytelling</u>, (Libraries Unlimited 2009)
- "Cougar on the Roof" is also based on multiple oral histories I have collected over the years.
- "The Seed" is from my book <u>Learning From the Land</u>, (Libraries Unlimited 2012)
- "The Blue Crawfish" is an original story, first published here. It was inspired in a writing workshop I lead for students and was recently proofread by Caitlin Bloomer, a graduate student studying burrowing crayfish.
- "Three Folktales About Flowers" is an original weaving of my love for prairie wildflowers with snippets of Lakota folktales from <u>Prairie Smoke</u> by Melvin R. Gilmore, first published in 1929, reprinted by Minnesota Historical Society Press, used with permission.

Brian "Fox" Ellis is an internationally acclaimed author, storyteller, historian, and naturalist. He has worked with The Abraham Lincoln Presidential Library and Museum, The Field Museum and dozens of other museums across the country. He has hosted, produced written and researched several documentaries for PBS and has recently launched a podcast Fox Tales International. He is the author of more than 2 dozen books including the critically acclaimed Learning From the Land: Teaching Ecology Through Stories and Activities, (Libraries Unlimited, 2011), a series of Chautauqua style autobiographies, *History In Person,* and this collection of *Fox Tales Folklore.* Many of his stories are also available on his YouTube channel *Fox Tales International.* He and his wife run a Bed and Breakfast in Bishop Hill, Illinois, The Twinflower Inn, where he also leads bird watching adventures and is replanting a prairie garden!

Devin McSherry is a freelance illustrator, hand-lettering artist, and surface pattern designer born and raised in the Prairie State of Illinois. Her best days are spent walking through nature, illustrating things that inspire her, cooking from scratch, and keeping her hands busy with sewing and other crafts. She's also learning to garden and enjoys getting involved with local permaculture-focused organizations. She currently lives alongside her husband, Ryan, in the suburbs of Chicago. Are you interested in working with Devin on your next creative project? You can view more of her work by visiting her website (www.devinmcsherry.com) and following her on Instagram (@devin.mcsherry).

This Book is part of a Multimedia Series Available at
www.foxtalesint.com
Visit this website to see the other books in the series.

If you purchased the audio book
and video here is your access code:

To watch a performance and listen to more
Fox Tales Folklore
in this series you can also subscribe to
the YouTube channel and podcast:

Fox Tales International